Neil Armstrong

By Dana Meachen Rau

Consultant
Jeanne Clidas, Ph.D.
National Reading Consultant
and
Professor of Reading, SUNY Brockport

◀P▶ Children's Press ®
A Division of Scholastic Inc.
New York   Toronto   London   Auckland   Sydney
Mexico City   New Delhi   Hong Kong
Danbury, Connecticut

Designer: Herman Adler Design
Photo Researcher: Caroline Anderson
The photo on the cover shows Neil Armstrong.

Library of Congress Cataloging-in-Publication Data

Rau, Dana Meachen, 1971-
  Neil Armstrong / by Dana Meachen Rau.
    p. cm. — (Rookie biographies)
Includes index.
Summary: An introduction to the life of astronaut Neil Armstrong, who
was the first man on the moon.
  ISBN 0-516-22592-8 (lib. bdg.)   0-516-26963-1 (pbk.)
  1. Armstrong, Neil, 1930—Juvenile literature. 2. Astronauts—United
States—Biography—Juvenile literature. [1. Armstrong, Neil, 1930- 2.
Astronauts.] I. Title. II. Series: Rookie biography.
  TL789.85.A75 R38 2003
  629.45'0092—dc21

                              2002015154

10 11 12 R 12   62

Do you like to explore new places?

A man named Neil Armstrong was an explorer. He visited a place no one had been before.

He went to the Moon!

Neil Armstrong was born
in Ohio on August 5, 1930.
He had one brother and
sister. He was the oldest.

Neil was always interested in flying. His house was filled with model airplanes. He built them himself.

Armstrong took flying lessons at an airport near his home. He became a pilot when he was only sixteen. He even studied flying in college.

He flew planes in the Korean (kor-EE-uhn) War in 1951. He was given medals for his good work.

He married Janet Shearon in 1956.

They had two sons.

Armstrong worked as a test pilot in California. He flew over 200 different rockets, helicopters, and jets.

One of the rocket planes Armstrong tested was called the X-15. It was the highest flying plane. It flew 40 miles high and reached speeds of 4,000 miles per hour.

The United States had a space program and wanted to send people to the Moon.

Armstrong was chosen to be one of the astronauts (AS-truh-nauts). He trained for four years before he could fly into space.

The first mission (MISH-uhn) Armstrong went on was *Gemini 8* in 1966. He and another astronaut had to hook up their spacecraft with a rocket already floating in space.

Their spacecraft spun out of control. Armstrong had to land fast! He stayed very calm.

Armstrong became the captain of the *Apollo 11* mission in 1969.

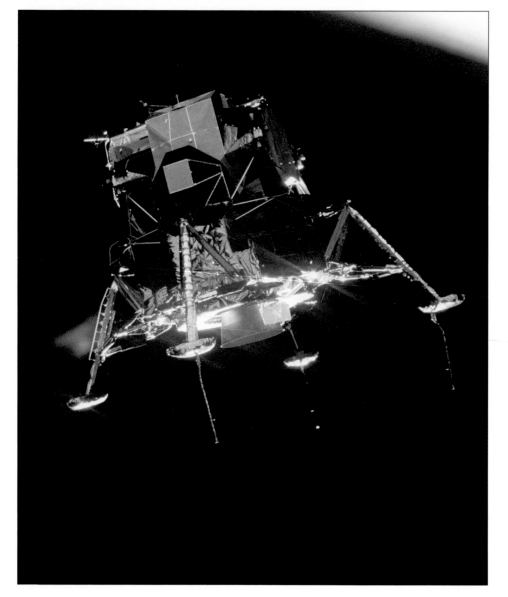

20

Armstrong and Buzz Aldrin landed on the Moon in a spacecraft called the *Eagle*. Then Armstrong became the first person to walk on the Moon.

Millions (MIL-yuhnz) of people watched him from Earth on television.

Armstrong and Aldrin collected Moon rocks and took pictures.

23

24

The astronauts made it home safely. There were parades and parties all over the world.

Armstrong became a teacher.
He taught at the University
of Cincinnati. Then he worked
in business.

Today, he lives in Ohio.

28

Armstrong always believed in following his dreams. He was the first person to explore a new and exciting world.

His footprint can still be found in the dust on the moon!

Words You Know

Neil Armstrong

astronaut

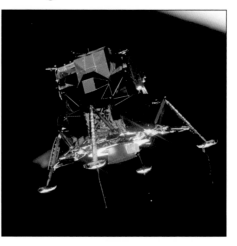

Eagle

explorer

Gemini 8

pilot

rocket plane

Index

About the Author

Dana Meachen Rau is the author of more than sixty books for children, including early readers, nonfiction, storybooks, and biographies. She also works as a children's book editor and illustrator. She looks at the moon through her telescope with her husband Chris, and children Charlie and Allison, in Farmington, Connecticut.

Photo Credits

Photographs © 2003: Corbis Images: 11 (Bettmann), 3, 31 top left (Layne Kennedy), 9; Getty Images: 7; NASA: 20, 30 bottom right (Michael Collins), 5, 23, 30 bottom left (Kennedy Space Center), cover, 12, 13, 15, 16, 17, 19, 22, 24, 28, 30 top, 31 top right, 31 bottom left, 31 bottom right; Stockphoto.com: 27 (Dennis Brack), 6, 10 (WBSS); Stockphoto.com: 27 (Dennis Brack), 6, 10 (WBSS).

Rookie biographies™

This Rookie Biography teaches young readers about Neil Armstrong, the astronaut who became famous as the commander of the *Apollo 11* spacecraft. Young readers will learn how he became a pilot at age 16 and went on to become one of the first men to walk on the Moon.

Read these other Rookie Biographies™

Abraham Lincoln	Jackie Robinson
Alexander Graham Bell	John Muir
Amelia Earhart	Johnny Appleseed
Benjamin Franklin	Laura Bush
Christopher Columbus	Laura Ingalls Wilder
Clara Barton	Mae Jemison
Dr. Seuss	Martin Luther King Jr.
George W. Bush	Pocahontas
George Washington	Rudolph Giuliani
Harriet Tubman	

U.S. $4.95
Can. $6.95

ISBN 0-516-26963-1

9 780516 269634

90000

CHILDREN'S PRESS

SCHOLASTIC